LIONEL MESSI: ALL YOU NEED TO KNOW ABOUT THE FOOTBALL LEGEND

LUIZ RIBEIRO

Table of Contents

The life of Lionel Messi

Lionel Andrés Messi, a football player for Argentina's national team and FC Barcelona in the Primera División, was born on June 24, 1987, in Rosario. He currently plays for Paris Saint-Germain. Messi is frequently referred to in the media as the "New Maradona," and Diego Maradona has publicly referred to Messi as his "successor."

Messi was born on June 24, 1987, in Rosario, Santa Fe. He is the third of four children and the husband of steel plant manager Jorge Messi and magnet factory worker Celia Cuccittini. He is the great-grandson of immigrants from Italy's north-western Adriatic Marche area on his father's side, and on his mother's side, he is predominantly of Italian lineage. Leo, who grew up in a close-knit football-loving family, became passionate about the game at a young age while playing with his older brothers Rodrigo and Matas, as well as his cousins Maximiliano and Emanuel Biancucchi, who both went on to play professionally. At the age of four, he joined the local team Grandoli, where his father served as his coach. However, his maternal grandmother Celia, who accompanied him to practice and games, had the earliest impact on his development as a player. His grandmother's passing, which occurred just before his eleventh birthday, had a significant impact on him. Ever since then, as a devoted Roman Catholic, he has celebrated his accomplishments by pointing to the sky in memory of his grandmother.

Messi became a member of the Rosario club when he was six years old and has been a longtime follower of Newell's Old Boys. As a member of "The Machine of '87," the nearly unstoppable youth squad named after the year they were born, he amused fans by performing ball tricks during halftime of the first team's home matches throughout the six years he played for Newell's. He also scored nearly 500 goals during that period. When he was diagnosed with a growth hormone shortage at age 10, it put his career as a professional player in jeopardy. The Newell's agreed to contribute because his father's health insurance would only pay for growth hormone therapy for two years, which would have cost at least $1,000 a month.

However, they eventually broke their word. He was discovered by Argentine team River Plate, whose playmaker Pablo Aimar he admired, but they refused to cover the cost of his medical care. Ronaldo was Messi's goal-scoring hero in his formative years; Messi referred to him as "the best forward I've ever seen."

The Messi family attempted to set up a trial with Barcelona in September 2000 since they had relatives living in Catalonia. The board of directors hesitated; at the time, it was quite unusual for European clubs to sign foreign players at such a young age. First team director Charly Rexach was immediately interested in signing him. Barcelona was given until December 14 to demonstrate their dedication, and Rexach offered a contract on a paper napkin because he was out of paper. The family went to Barcelona in February 2001, where they settled into an apartment close to the team's stadium, Camp Nou. Due to a transfer disagreement with Newell's, Messi had little action with the Infantiles during his first season in Spain; as a foreign player, he was only allowed to play in friendlies and the Catalan league. Without football, he found it difficult to fit in; already reticent by nature, he was so silent at first that his teammates thought he was deaf. After his mother moved back to Rosario with his brothers and little sister, Mara Sol, while he stayed in Barcelona with his father, he experienced longing at home.

In February 2002, Messi eventually signed up for the Royal Spanish Football Federation (RFEF) after spending a year at Barcelona's youth facility, La Masia. Now participating in all matches, he made friends with his colleagues, namely Cesc Fàbregas and Gerard Piqué. Messi joined the "Baby Dream Team," Barcelona's greatest-ever young team, when he finished his growth hormone therapy at the age of 14. In his first full season (2002–03), the Cadetes A accomplished an unprecedented treble by winning the league, the Spanish Cup, and the Catalan Cup, and he led the team in scoring with 36 goals in 30 games. The Copa Catalunya championship game, which Barcelona won 4-1 over Espanyol, earned the nickname "partido de la máscara," or "mask final," in club legend. A week after breaking his cheekbone during a league game, Messi was permitted to start the game under the condition that he wear a plastic protector; nevertheless, after finding the mask to be a hindrance, he removed it and went on to score two goals in 10 minutes before being replaced. He received his first offer from a foreign team to join Arsenal at the end of the season, but he decided to stay in Barcelona while Fàbregas and Piqué soon went for England.

Messi quickly rose through the ranks of the club during the 2003–04 season, his fourth with Barcelona, making his debut for a record five youth teams in a single season.

He played just one official game with the Juveniles B after winning player of the tournament honors in four international preseason tournaments with the squad before being promoted to the Juveniles A, where he scored 18 goals in 11 league games. Then, during the international break, Messi was one of several young players called in to bolster a thin first team. Messi drew the attention of Frank Rijkaard's first squad during a training session, according to French winger Ludovic Giuly: "He

made us all nothing... To escape being made fun
of by this boy, they were kicking him all over
the place, but he just rose up and carried on
playing. He would make a goal by dribbling past
four opponents. Even the starting center backs
for the club were uneasy. He was a foreigner."

Messi made his first team debut on November
16, 2003, against José Mourinho's Porto in a
friendly at the age of 16 years, 4 months, and 23
days. The technical staff was impressed with his
performance, which resulted in two chances and
a shot on goal. As a result, he started working
out every day with Barcelona B, the club's
reserve team, in addition to once a week with the
first squad. Barça's new star player, Ronaldinho,
informed his colleagues during his first practice
with the senior team that he thought the 16-year-
old will develop into an even better player than
himself. Ronaldinho quickly made friends with
Messi, whom he referred to as his "little

brother," which made it much easier for him to make the first team.

Messi joined Barcelona C in addition to the Juveniles A to get more match experience, and on November 29, he played his first game for the third level. With five goals in ten games, including a hat-trick in eight minutes during a Copa del Rey encounter while being man-marked by Sergio Ramos of Sevilla, he helped keep them out of the Tercera División's relegation zone. His first professional contract, which he signed on February 4th, 2004, ran until 2012 and had a €30 million buyout clause, highlighted his advancement. His buyout clause immediately increased to €80 million when he made his debut for Barcelona B in the Segunda División B one month later, on March 6. He didn't score in his five games with the B team that season. He was physically inferior to his opponents, who were frequently older and taller. In order to overcome this disadvantage, he trained to build up his muscle mass and overall strength. He joined both youth teams again toward the end of the campaign, which helped the Juveniles B win the league. He concluded the season with 36 goals across all official competitions, scoring for four of his five sides.

Messi was a sure starter for the B squad during the 2004–05 season, appearing in 17 games and tallying six goals. He had not been called up to the first team since his debut in November of the previous year, but in October 2004, the senior players petitioned manager Frank Rijkaard to promote him. Although originally against the player's preferences, Rijkaard shifted Messi from his customary position to the right side because Ronaldinho was already playing on the left wing. This allowed Messi to cut into the middle of the field and shoot with his left foot, which is his dominant foot. Messi entered the game against Espanyol in the 82nd minute to make his league debut. That game took place on October 16. He was at the time the youngest player to represent Barcelona in a formal match at the age of 17 years, three months, and 22 days. He appeared in nine games for the first team that season as a substitute and completed 244 minutes of action, making his UEFA Champions League debut against Shakhtar Donetsk. On May 1, 2005, against Albacete, he scored his first goal as a senior off an assist from Ronaldinho, making him the club's youngest-ever goal scorer at the moment. For the first time in six years, Barcelona won the league in their second season under Rijkaard.

Messi signed his first contract as a senior team member on June 24, the day before his 18th birthday. It reduced the length of his Barcelona deal by two years to 2010 while raising the buyout clause to €150 million. Two months later, on August 24, he made his breakthrough at the Joan Gamper Trophy, a preseason match for Barcelona. He made his debut start against Juventus under Fabio Capello, and the Camp Nou cheered him on for his performance. While Capello asked for Messi to be on loan, Inter Milan made a purchase offer, offering to pay his €150 million buyout clause and triple his salary.

It was the only occasion when the club truly ran the risk of losing Messi, but he ultimately chose to stay, according to the club's then-president Joan Laporta. His contract was revised for the second time in three months on September 16 and was extended through 2014.

Messi missed the start of La Liga due to concerns with his legal standing in the Royal Spanish Football Federation, but on September 26, he obtained Spanish citizenship and qualified to participate. He gradually made himself the first-choice right winger while donning the number 19 jersey, forming an attacking combination alongside Ronaldinho and striker Samuel Eto'o. He started important games like the first Clásico he played in on November 19 against rival Real Madrid and Barcelona's away win over Chelsea in the Champions League's round of 16. The matchup came after a heated period of rivalry between the two teams, which led a resentful Messi to say, "We would rather play Arsenal, Manchester United, or anyone else than be on the field with Chelsea." After amassing 8 goals in 25 games, including his first Champions League goal in a 5-0 victory over

Panathinaikos on 2 November 2005, his season was cut short early on 7 March 2006 when he tore his hamstring in the second leg against Chelsea. Messi put forth effort to get back in shape for the Champions League final, but on May 17, the day of the final, he was ultimately disqualified. He was so angry that he did not rejoice when his team beat Arsenal in Paris, which he later regretted.

The 2006–07 season saw Messi, then 19 years old, establish himself as one of the best players in the world, while Barcelona began a slow decline. He had already established himself as the club's idol after scoring 17 goals in 36 games across all competitions. However, he kept suffering serious wounds; a metatarsal fracture he suffered on November 12, 2006, forced him to miss three months of play. Although he returned in time for the Champions League match against Liverpool in the round of 16, Barcelona, the defending champions, had already exited the competition. As the season came to a close, his league goal output grew; 11 of his 14 goals came from the final 13 games. He became the first player in 12 years to score a hat-trick in a Clásico on March 10, 2007, tying the score after each Real Madrid goal to conclude the game in a 3-3 tie. His increasing value to the team was reflected in a new contract that month that significantly raised his pay.

World Records Messi Holds

Every football fan in the world experiences sadness when a player departs the Barcelona football club. During his more than 20 years of playing for Barcelona, Messi sets numerous records.

All of the significant records in FC Barcelona's past are held by the Argentine superstar. He has played for the team the most times. He has amassed the most goals and victories. And maybe most significantly, in the 121-year history of the club, he has won the most championships.

World Records for Lionel Messi

• The only player in history to win the Golden Boot, Pichichi Trophy, FIFA World Player, and Ballon d'Or all in the same year. It took place during the 2009–10 campaign.

• The athlete who has won the most Ballons d'Or. Six victories have been his. 2009, 2010, 2011, 2012, 2015, and 2019 saw their arrival.

• Athlete to receive three Ballons d'Or at a young age. He won the third on January 9, 2012, at the age of 24 years, 6 months, and 17 days.

• The participant with the most Golden Shoes. won six times. The 2009–10, 2011–12, 2012–13, 2016–17, 2017–18, and 2018–19 seasons saw them.

• Season's top scorer in official contests. He was the all-time leading scorer in a calendar year with 73 goals in 2011–12 (50 in the league, 14 in the Champions League, 3 in the Copa del Rey, 3 in the Spanish Super Cup, 1 in the European Super Cup, and 2 in the Club World Cup). He registered 91 goals in 2012. 12 with the Argentine national team and 84 with Barça (59 in the league, 13 in the Champions League, 5 in the Copa del Rey, and 2 in the Super Cup).

•

Additionally, he scored 5 more goals in friendlies against Barça, bringing his career total of goals scored to 96.

• A year's worth of international goals. His 2012 total of 25 goals (13 in the Champions League and 12 with the Argentine national team) tied Vivian John Woodward's record of 25 goals in 1909 (25).

• Leading scorer for the same team He has 672 goals as of May 27, surpassing Pelé's 643 goals with Santos between 1956 and 1974.

• The league's longest scoring streak. In the 2012–13 league season, he scored 33 goals in 21 straight games from matchday 11 to matchday 34.

Luis Messi Records from Europe

Since the Golden Shoe trophy's inception in the 1966–1967 season, the player with the most goals in a European League. By scoring 50 goals in La Liga in 2011–12, you broke the record.

• The player with the most goals in the Champions League against various opponents. He has scored more goals than Cristiano Ronaldo (35), who has faced 36 different opponents.

Luis Messi Records in Spanish

• The athlete with the most national and international championships. Since 2002, he has 35. Ten leagues, eight Spanish Super Cups, seven Copa del Reys, four Champions Leagues, three Club World Cups, and three European Super Cups are available.

• The Spanish league player with the most Pichichi Trophies. He has achieved 87 victories. In the 2009–10, 2011–12, 212–13, 2016–17, 2017–18, 2018–19, 2019–20, and 2020–21 seasons, he carried it out.

• The Spanish League's leading scorer. He had scored 474 goals in 520 games as of May 27, 2021.

• All-time leading scorer. On May 27, 2021, he had 709 points in 836 contests.

• The top scoring in sanctioned events. He currently has 672 goals as of May 27, 2021.

• International competitions' top scorer. He has scored 128 goals in all, including 120 in the Champions League, three in the European Super Cup, and five in the Club World Cup.

• Top scorer in any LA Liga season. scored 50 goals in the league in 2011–2012.

• Top scorer for official matches played at home in a season: During the 2011–12 season, Leo Messi scored 46 goals at the Camp Nou across all competitions.

• Top domestic scorer in a LA Liga season. He scored 35 goals at Camp Nou during the league season 2011–2012.

• The top LA Liga scorer during a season away from home. scored 24 away goals during the league season of 2012–2013.

• Most goals scored in consecutive away league games. In 15 straight away games during the 2012–13 league season, he scored 24 goals.

• Leading scorer in Laila's round two. tallied 28 goals in the second half of the league season in 2011–12.

• The only player to have led the league in both scoring and assists in the same campaign. In the 2011–12 league season, he tied Real Madrid player Zil with 50 goals and 15 assists. Additionally, he did it in the 2017–18 league season (34 goals and 12 assists, tied with Luis Suárez in goals and Pablo Fornals of Villarreal in assists), as well as the 2019–29 league season (25 goals and 21 assists).

• Season's leading scorer by a wide margin. In the 2011–12 season, he scored 73 goals (50 in the league, 14 in the Champions League, three in the Cup, three in the Spanish Super Cup, one in the European Super Cup, and two in the Club World Cup), in addition to two additional goals in friendlies.

• The majority of goals scored during a league season. He equalled Cristiano Ronaldo of Real Madrid, who also scored in 27 games in the 2011–12 season, by scoring in 27 separate league games in the 2012–13 season (46 goals).

• The first player to score during an entire round of a league game. In the 2012–13 season, he scored 30 goals in 19 straight games, between days 11 and 29.

• The player that contributed the most hat tricks, four-goal games, and five-goal games throughout official competition. On March 22, 2021, he has 48. (41 hat-tricks, 6 four-goal hauls and one five-goal game).

The league player with the most hat tricks and four goals scored is 36. Over the course of his career, he has scored five four-goal hauls and a total of 31 hat tricks in LA Liga.

• The entire league season with all opponents scoring. He equalled Cristiano Ronaldo of Real Madrid's 2011–12 LA Liga scoring record by scoring against every team during the 2012–13 LA Liga season.

• A player with a high scoring rate in La Liga. In the Spanish top division, he has scored against 38 different opponents, breaking Ral González and Aritz Aduriz's previous record of 35.

The La Liga player with the most direct free-kick goals. In the league, he has scored off of 38 direct free kicks.

• The competitor with the most victories in a formal match. A total of 542 victories as of May 27, 2021. Xavi is in second place with 476 triumphs.

• The Spanish league's most successful player. He had 383 victories in the domestic competition as of May 27, 2021.

• The player with the most El Clásico appearances. He has played 45 games versus Real Madrid as of May 27, 2021. (29 in the league, 8 in the Copa del Rey, 2 in the

Champions League and 6 in the Spanish
Super Cup).

• The El Clásico player with the most goals.
He has scored 26 goals against Real Madrid
as of May 27, 2021. (18 in LA Liga, 2 in the
Champions League and 6 in the Spanish
Super Cup).

Personal records for Lionel Messi at
Barcelona

• The participant with the most official
games. He had played 778 games as of May
27, 2021, since his official debut.

• The national team player who has made the
most appearances for Argentina. He has
played for Argentina 148 times as of June
29th, breaking Javier Mascherano's previous
mark of 147.

• The player who has participated in the most
league games. Since making his official
debut in October 2004, he has played 520
games as of May 27, 2021.

• The player that scored 100 goals in a career at the earliest age. On January 16, 2010, when he was 22 years old, he attained the milestone.

• The player who scored 200 goals in a career's earliest matches. On November 1, 2011, when he was 24 years old, he attained the milestone.

• Leading scorer in the Champions League or European Cup. Nearly 100 more than all of his main pursuers, he has 120 goals.

• The only player in club history to score in six legitimate tournaments in a calendar year. In 2011, Messi scored in each of the six games, matching Pedro Rodriguez's accomplishment from 2009.

• The player who scored the most goals during a certain Champions League season. In the 2011–12 Champions League, Leo Messi scored 14 goals. Cristiano Ronaldo set the record for the competition in 2013/14, making it to 17.

Messi's Earnings

Lionel Messi, the captain of Argentina's national football team, is regarded as one of the best players in the world. He previously played for the Spanish club Barcelona and is currently a member of Paris Saint-Germain. He's in great shape right now. In the last three games for Argentina, he has scored nine goals. He also became one of the athletes with 100 international victories. In addition to this, he also played international football and scored 90 goals. When it comes to players with the most goals, he is third.

Messi is renowned for both his outstanding play and his success. His most recent Ballon d'Or victory set a record. He is the athlete who has won this prize the most frequently. Read this chapter through to the finish because we will inform you of Lionel Messi's 2022 Net Worth and Earnings.

According to Forbes' list of highest-paid athletes, Lionel Messi comes in first place. 130 million US dollars are his annual earnings. Of this, 55 million US dollars have been made outside of sports, leaving 75 million US dollars to be made through sports. Lionel Messi is reportedly the richest football player in the world with a net worth of over 620 million US dollars.

His wage in Paris St. German, where he arrived in 2021 after leaving Barcelona, is 22 million dollars less than it was in Barcelona. His wages have grown despite this. Through various strategies, including advertising, he has raised his income. Messi promotes a number of well-known brands, such as Lay's, Pepsi, and Adidas.

Awesome Facts About Messi

1) Jorge Messi, the father of Lionel Andrés Messi, was a steelworker and the head coach of the neighborhood youth football club.
2) Messi and Argentine revolutionary Che Guevera were both born in the same city.

3) At the age of four, he joined the local team Grandoli, where his father served as his coach. However, his maternal grandmother Celia, who accompanied him to practice and games, had the greatest impact on his development as a player.

4) Her passing, which occurred just before his eleventh birthday, had a significant impact on him; ever since, as a devout Catholic, he has celebrated his accomplishments by pointing to the sky in memory of his grandmother.

5) Messi was diagnosed with a growth hormone deficit at the tender age of 11, which was slowing his normal pace of growth.

His treatment cost $1000 a month, which his parents could not afford.

6) The Barcelona First Team Director Charly Rexach quickly wanted to recruit him in September 2000, but the club's board of directors held off because it was extremely uncommon for European clubs to sign foreign players at such a young age at the time.

7) Messi's first Barcelona contract was written out in full on a paper napkin!

8) He made his league debut at the age of 17 against RCD Espanyol, becoming him the third-youngest player in Barcelona history. He was also the youngest player to have ever scored for Barcelona at the time.

9) Barcelona offered to cover Messi's medical fees and move the family to Spain simply to sign him when he was 13 because they were so impressed with his footwork. That most likely explains why the contract was initially signed on a piece of paper.

10) On November 2, 2012, he gave birth to a son named Thiago. He posted on his Facebook page, "Today I am the happiest guy in the world, my son was born and gratitude to God for this gift!"

11) Messi is a dual citizen of Argentina and Spain. In September 2005, he attained Spanish nationality.

12) His 2005 international debut was cut short after 47 seconds due to a red card after being substituted in.

13) In the summer of 2008, Messi acquired the No. 10 Barcelona jersey from another legendary footballer, Ronaldinho.

14) He won an Olympic gold medal with the Argentinian football team at the Beijing Olympics in 2008.

15) Messi won his first FIFA World Player of the Year honor at the age of 22. Following that, he made an attempt to hold onto that prize by winning it for the following three years.

16) Messi became the youngest player to score 200 goals in the Spanish La Liga at the age of 25, accomplishing the feat.

17) Messi is the only player to have scored 25 goals in a calendar year while competing for

both his club and his country, together with England's Vivian Woodward.

18) Messi once turned down an invitation to play for Spain's national team.

Messi, 19, is the sixth-youngest player in World Cup history to score a goal.

20) Because of his quickness and dexterity, Messi goes by the moniker "The Flea."

21) Barcelona will be required to pay more than $330 million as compensation for breach of contract if, for any reason, they decide to terminate their agreement with Lionel Messi.

22) Messi is presently the second-richest player in the world, behind Cristiano Ronaldo, according to Forbes, who has a net worth of $180 million.

23) He may earn up to $128,000 per day, including endorsements and contracts, according to Complex.com.

24) He has won three European Golden Shoe Awards, making him the first football player in history to do so.

25) He is the only football player in history to receive three European Golden Shoes.

He has the most hat-tricks at Barcelona (number 26).

27) In 2012, Messi scored 91 goals. That sets a new record for the most goals in a calendar year.

28) Since 2009, he has been seeing Antonella Roccuzzo, the mother of his child and an Argentinean-born girlfriend.

Messi And the World Cup 2022

At the FIFA World Cup 2022 final between France and Argentina on Sunday at the Lusail Stadium, Argentina's captain Lionel Messi broke numerous records. Messi is the only male player to ever participate in every round of a single FIFA World Cup.

Lionel Messi, who will captain two-time champions Argentina in the FIFA World Cup 2022 championship match on Sunday, has broken a tremendous record by surpassing German legend Lothar Matthaus on an exclusive list. When Argentina and France met in the Qatar Global Cup final at the Lusail Stadium, one of the greatest players in the history of the "beautiful game" Messi set a world record. Argentina's captain Messi has made his 26th appearance at the FIFA World Cup, making him one of only six players to do so. The 35-year-old is now the player with the most FIFA World Cup appearances, surpassing Germany's Matthaus. The talisman of Argentina has played more games than any other player in the history of the premier competition. The seven-time Ballon d'Or winner recently broke Gabriel Batistuta's record during the semi-final round of

the coveted competition, rewriting history for the FIFA World Cup 2022.
Argentina defeated Croatia 3-0 in the FIFA World Cup semi-finals, with Messi scoring for the two-time champions. With his 11th goal for Argentina in the FIFA World Cup, the 35-year-old passed Batistuta in terms of World Cup goals. The charismatic captain of La Albiceleste now holds the FIFA World Cup record for most goals scored by an Argentine player (11).
Messi currently holds the record for the most FIFA World Cup minutes played. Messi has eclipsed Paolo Maldini, an Italian icon who played 2,217 minutes during the FIFA World Cup. Maldini was overtaken by Messi in the opening period of the FIFA World Cup 2022 final, making history. Messi has made 19 appearances as captain in the FIFA World Cup since making his debut on the biggest platform in 2006.
Rafa Marquez (17) and Diego Maradona follow the South American giants' all-time leading goal scorer (16). Only Messi has a World Cup assist in five different tournaments. When the Argentina captain scored his sixth goal to put his team ahead early in the final, he broke the record for most goals scored at the Qatar World Cup. Messi is the only male player to ever participate

in every round of a single FIFA World Cup.
After losing their initial match, Messi's
Argentina team is attempting to become the
second team in World Cup history to win the
coveted title. The less well-known achievement
was accomplished by former winners Spain in
the 2010 FIFA World Cup.

At Qatar 2022, Lionel Messi was named the best
player.

For the first time ever, a man has won multiple
adidas Golden Balls.

The Silver and Bronze Balls were won by
Kylian Mbappe and Luka Modric, respectively.

At the FIFA World Cup, Lionel Messi made
history by being the first person to ever win the
adidas Golden Ball twice. At Qatar 2022, "La
Pulga Atomica" helped Argentina win the trophy
for the first time in 32 years by scoring seven
goals and dishing out three assists while setting
numerous records.

The Silver Ball was awarded to Kylian Mbappe,
and the Bronze Ball was given to Luka Modric.